ZEN ~as~ F*CK AT WORK

A JOURNAL FOR BANISHING THE BULLSH*T AND FINDING CALM IN THE CHAOS

Monica Sweeney

CASTLE POINT BOOKS

NEW YORK

THIS BOOK BELONGS TO:

HAPPY FUCKING MONDAY!

Welcome to your brand-new workday. It's a hotbed of hope, a shining beacon on the horizon of a soul-crushing landscape of responsibility. On each page of this journal is a guided prompt that lets you cast off workplace calamities, ditch the drama, and soothe the shit that stresses you out with tons of serenity.

Start your workday off right with a few moments of positive profanity, take a bliss break from the 9-to-5 grind, and learn to embrace off-grid off-hours so you feel refreshed as fuck. With some upbeat contemplation and a no-fucks-given attitude, you can find some tranquility in all that turmoil and focus on what makes your world bright. Find vibrancy in your vocation and get inspired by all that lies ahead.

Boss up, employ your joy, and make work fucking great!

BANISH *the* BULLSHIT

No job is without its nonsense. Whether you work in an office, with your hands, or as the noble thrill-seeker who changes the lightbulbs at the tops of cell phone towers, you deal with some serious bullshit on a day-to-day basis. What do you want to say to that BS?

Write it out here.

_____

_____

_____

_____

_____

_____

_____

_____

_____

_____

_____

_____

_____

"Downtime for the human operating system is not a bug, it's a feature."

—ARIANNA HUFFINGTON, *WORK LIFE*

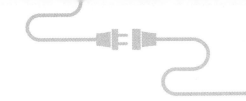

BE YOUR OWN GENIUS BAR

Plugging away and working yourself to the bone may **seem** like the can-do qualities of the next Employee of the Month, but the reality is your body needs some downtime. Treat your body like your internet router—if it stops working, unplug the fucking thing and wait a while before restarting. It almost always works!

Whether it's five minutes or five hours—what are a few things you can do during or after the work day to help you feel refreshed?

_____

_____

_____

_____

_____

_____

_____

How does it feel when you

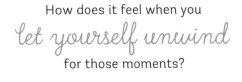

let yourself unwind

for those moments?

"I was a little excited but mostly blorft.

'BLORFT' IS AN ADJECTIVE I JUST MADE UP

that means 'Completely overwhelmed but

PROCEEDING AS IF EVERYTHING IS FINE

and reacting to the stress with

THE TORPOR OF A POSSUM.'"

— BOSSYPANTS, TINA FEY

I'M SORRY, BUT I'M JUST FEELING VERY BLORFT RIGHT NOW

There is that special kind of work stress that is so overwhelming, so unapproachable, that the only reasonable reaction is to burrow into a hole and stress-nap until maybe it goes away. Unfortunately, that stress will still be there to scare the everliving shit out of you when you crawl out of said hole. Instead of being scared of it, make fun of it before you kick its ass.

Make up your own silly adjectives

for when you're feeling overwhelmed.

_____   _____

_____   _____

_____   _____

_____   _____

_____   _____

Shout them out as loud as you can when you've hit your limit. It won't fix the problem, but it'll give you a second of relief before you get back at it!

COMPLIMENTS on RYE

The "feedback sandwich," a method for delivering bad news or negative feedback by sandwiching it between two slices of praise, is usually something you serve up to other people. But why does everyone else get to have the delicious, self-bettering sandwich? If you're feeling like you did a trash job on something, let yourself look at the positive pieces that balance out the junk.

What went well?

_____

_____

_____

_____

What aspects can you carry over when you try again?

_____

_____

_____

_____

ADDRESS WHAT YOU NEED TO FIX, BUT DON'T FORGET TO PRAISE YOURSELF FOR THAT GOOD, GOOD BREAD.

BOB PORTER:
Looks like you've been
missing a lot of work lately.

PETER GIBBONS:
I wouldn't say I've been missing it, Bob.

—*OFFICE SPACE*

SORRY I MISSED YOUR CALL

Shirking your responsibilities: Not great. Remembering that you don't always have to take work home with you: Amazing! If you are someone who checks email after hours, sticks around the office longer than you should, or someone who even thinks about those fucking TPS reports when you're supposed to be spending time with loved ones or binging valuable streaming services, try adding up exactly how much time you do that in a given night.

What can you do in place of those added work hours that will help you truly unwind?

_____

_____

_____

_____

_____

_____

_____

MY REIGN HAS
JUST BEGUN.

—DAENERYS TARGARYEN, *GAME OF THRONES*

SET EVERYTHING ON FIRE

Aren't metaphors fun? Instead of actually burning everything to the ground (because that's some next-level scary shit), set some intentions instead. Make a list of 5-10 things that usually make you breathe fire in the left-hand column. In the opposite column, write the ways you can let that shit float away from you like smoke and embers in the night sky.

AM I ZEN YET?

ZENTASTIC!

You can't become your very own chill-as-fuck work guru without trying to offset your stress. When pressure starts to encroach on you and your day, step out of your workspace and allow yourself a calming activity. Sip tea slowly, go for a walk, or do a quick dance under some lavender air freshener and pretend you're in a fucking field.

How does it feel?

_____

_____

_____

_____

How would it feel to use that ritual regularly?

_____

_____

_____

_____

Whatever it is, let that moment be yours and yours only.

MORNING RITUAL, 2.0

Rise and shine, friendo. Start your morning with stillness. Sit up in bed and set your alarm for 10 minutes of peace with your eyes closed. Let the 10 minutes pass by without interruption, keeping your breathing even. When you start to flip out because you haven't looked at your phone in a few minutes—calm the hell down, it's right next to you—breathe in slowly. Do this a few mornings in a row and come back to this page each time.

How does sitting still make you feel?

_____

_____

_____

_____

_____

_____

_____

What does this extra 10 minutes do for your day before you get to the grind?

"I recently went into my boss's office to ask for a raise, and it felt really confrontational, so I just quit."

—EMILY WINTER, *WORK LIFE*

HOW TO ASK FOR A RAISE

ASK for THAT GOOD SHIT

What are you looking for at work? Whether it's a raise, more flexibility, or more high fives, half the battle of getting what you want is asking for it. (The other half is doing the work, *womp*.) How likely is it that you'll get fired for asking for these things? If it's likely, then you're probably asking for the wrong thing, or you work for a maniac (in which case you should actually quit). But since it's probably unlikely, write out how you could ask for it. Even if they say no, how will it feel to have made your needs known?

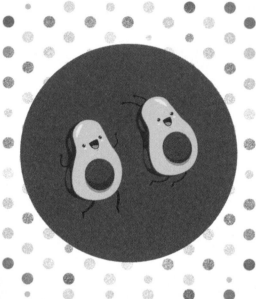

TRUST FALL!

Trusting others at work is a big ol' crapshoot. One train wreck can affirm negative trust behavior in which you refuse to let others help because you figure you can do it better yourself. But sometimes your trust in others has an amazing ROI, whether it's a colleague pulling through in the clutch, or merely helping you get some shit off your plate so you can breathe easier.

HOW CAN YOU BE MORE TRUSTING WHEN ASKING FOR WORK HELP?

IN WHAT WAYS DO OTHERS HAVE TRUST IN YOU?

DON'T LET THE TERRORISTS WIN

Most work environments have their saboteurs. (If you don't know who it is, it might be you. Why are you so mean?) The person who always undercuts other people's efforts, takes credit for their colleagues' hard work, or who makes everyone's lives miserable by not doing their own. When this person engages in work warfare, how can you respond?

Circle One:

A) Encourage the torture by helping them

B) Give up because *lol, oh well*

C) Reject their bad behavior

IF YOU ANSWERED A: No! Honestly, B isn't even a bad choice because at least you've stopped caring, but it does mean the pattern will continue. But C will help others in addition to helping you. Whether it's speaking up (diplomatically) or being the change you want to see at your work, spread the good behavior! Reject the bad! How do you think this will feel?

_____

_____

_____

_____

_____

_____

VLADISLAV:
Leave me to do my dark
bidding on the Internet!

VIAGO:
What are you bidding on?

VLADISLAV:
I am bidding on a table.

—*WHAT WE DO IN THE SHADOWS*

INTERNET, BE DAMNED!

Hey little Internet, you're so cute and distracting. A few li'l clicky-clicks of our friend The Web, and all of a sudden you have a full cart, you're several layers deep into a discussion forum conspiracy theory, and you've redesigned your life goals based on an influencer's super-legit success story. For the work that will allow it: Try turning off your WiFi, deactivating your notifications, or blocking yourself from certain websites so you can actually concentrate.

Commit to this for a trial period. How did taking those distractions away help you get work done?

_____

_____

_____

_____

Did you start to feel less frazzled because you weren't jumping from one thing to another?

_____

_____

_____

_____

ADMIRATION!

Who is someone you admire at your work? The person from whom you are eager to learn, whose presence is calming, or who always seems to know the right solution. Write about how this person improves your day. When you're finished, withhold this knowledge forever and never tell them.

(You should tell them.)

VICTORY!

In the 30 spaces below, write down one thing every day that went well at work. A compliment, a success, or a check mark indicating that you made it through eight hours without quiet-crying in the bathroom—use this opportunity to collect your victories.

1. _____

2. _____

3. _____

4. _____

5. _____

6. _____

7. _____

8. _____

9. _____

10. _____

11. _____

12. _____

13. _____

14. _____

15. _____

16. _____

17. _____

18. _____

19. _____

20. _____

21. _____

22. _____

23. _____

24. _____

25. _____

26. _____

27. _____

28. _____

29. _____

30. _____

Keep these positive reminders within reach

because you're doing fucking great!

SHRED *that* SHIT

Make a list of the frustrating things that happened recently that upset you at work: A comment by a colleague, an avoidable mistake, or something that royally effed up your day. Now, cross them out, shred them, or give them a pleasant burial in a trash can. Symbolic acts of dispatching your woes to their mortal ends help move past them, while opening up emotional space for something way better.

_____

_____

_____

_____

_____

_____

_____

_____

_____

_____

"Just because someone you work with is a miserable, treacherous, self-serving, capricious, and corrupt asshole shouldn't prevent you from enjoying their company, working with them, or finding them entertaining."

– *KITCHEN CONFIDENTIAL*, ANTHONY BOURDAIN

PEOPLE *have* WEAKNESSES

The hell-beast in your office or the killjoy on your conference call didn't get that way overnight. Are these people actually horrible, or are they just having a shitty go of it?

_____

_____

_____

_____

_____

What are some of their weaknesses that could be diffused with a little compassion, or that you could learn to ignore completely?

_____

_____

_____

_____

_____

ONE TRILLION VACATION DAYS

Not all vacation time is created equal. In some fields, you're shit out of luck if you want time off and have to go unpaid, and in others, you're given "unlimited" vacation time under the guise of *laissez-faire* benefits, but really you should have your ass in that chair if you want to keep your job. Imagine those vacation days were truly unfettered and you could use them without judgment.

IMAGINE YOUR IDEAL, NO-STRINGS VACATION DAYS ON THIS PAGE AND SOAK UP THEIR JOY.

HIDE YOUR STASH

Wherever you do your work, hide a secret stash of positivity to look to whenever you need to feel a sense of calm. A picture of a tranquil beach, a token from a good day with a friend or significant other, or a snow globe with an image of a cutie pup-pup in it—pull this out whenever you need to prevent yourself from losing your shit.

What would you use?

_____

_____

_____

_____

_____

_____

_____

_____

_____

_____

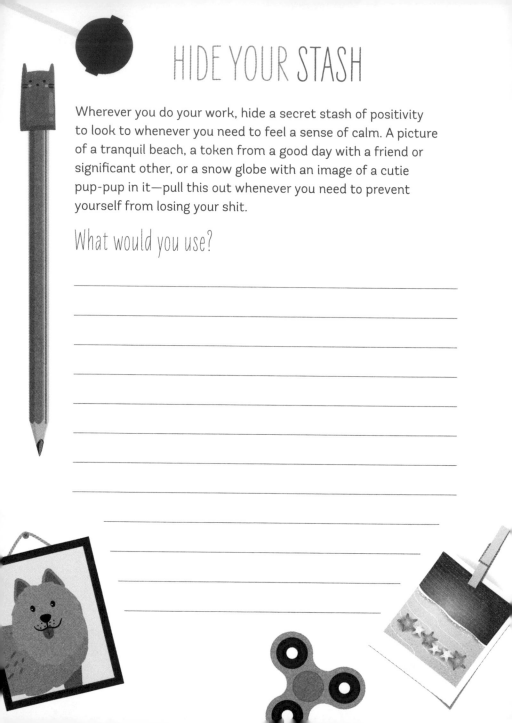

How does your emergency stash help?

I love you! ♡

"WE CAN NEVER GIVE UP LONGING AND WISHING
WHILE WE ARE THOROUGHLY ALIVE. THERE ARE
CERTAIN THINGS WE FEEL TO BE BEAUTIFUL AND
GOOD, AND WE MUST HUNGER AFTER THEM."

— *THE MILL ON THE FLOSS*, GEORGE ELIOT

WISHING and HOPING
and DREAMING

What are your water cooler wishes? Some people long for the kind of passion for their job that brings a sense of fulfillment, and others long for the kind of job that allows them time outside of it to fulfill their passions. (And others wish to be an eccentric billionaire and feel passionately about that, which is totally fine.)

What about these wishes brings you excitement?

_____

_____

_____

_____

What small steps can you take to get started?

_____

_____

_____

_____

_____

"TO ERR IS HUMAN, BUT
TO REALLY FOUL THINGS UP
REQUIRES A COMPUTER."

—PAUL EHRLICH

WHY DO YOU REFUSE *to* LEARN NEW TECHNOLOGY?!

Write a fake letter to that sweet, precious, very wonderful colleague or sworn enemy of yours who insists on being the 8-track to your cloud data. Unleash your wrath upon this page, or imagine what it would be like if they suddenly gave a fuck. Now, dance to the wireless sound of success!

_____

_____

_____

_____

_____

_____

_____

_____

_____

_____

There, there! It's going to be okay.

"'YES' SHOULD
FEEL LIKE
THE SUN."

— *YEAR OF YES*, SHONDA RHIMES

THE PINNACLE of YES

What opportunities have you shut down because they felt like a pain in the ass, too risky, or too high of a hill to climb? Is it an Everest of a challenge (over-trekked, littered with corpses, and maybe not worth it), or would the summit be transcendent and put you closer to the sun? Whether it's a new responsibility, coffee with a colleague you haven't yet gotten to know, or volunteering for something a little bit out of your comfort zone, what's preventing you from turning that no into a yes?

SAY N'NIGHT, NEGATIVITY!

Some people radiate negativity. They carry it around like some gross medieval disease that spreads to everything they touch, and suddenly there's a fucking plague of bad juju festering around you. Be a pioneer of positivity and cleanse that plague away. How can you immunize yourself from those bad vibes?

_____

_____

_____

_____

_____

_____

_____

_____

_____

_____

_____

_____

_____

"You know, it's funny...
when you look at someone
through rose-colored
glasses, all the red flags
just look like flags."

— WANDA PIERCE, *BOJACK HORSEMAN*

EVERYTHING'S COMING UP ROSES

Seeing the positives in people is super important! It creates a healthy environment of trust, empowerment, and success. But when someone is waving a million little red flags at you and all you see is a pretty great candidate for color guard, you may be in for disappointment.

When have you seen red flags in the past and ignored them?

What could have helped in that situation?

"WOULD I RATHER BE FEARED OR LOVED?
EASY—BOTH. I WANT PEOPLE TO BE
AFRAID OF HOW MUCH THEY LOVE ME."

—MICHAEL SCOTT, *THE OFFICE*

FEARLESS LEADER

Leaders come in a variety of forms. The big-wig boss, the colleague who seems to always have their shit together, or the person who leads the way to happy hour after work—different strengths span a broad, shimmering spectrum.

In what ways do you lead?

_____

_____

_____

_____

_____

_____

What kind of leadership do you love most?

_____

_____

_____

_____

_____

_____

"Auto-reply:
I am dead and will have
limited access to e-mail."

—TOM TORO, *THE NEW YORKER*

AUTO-REPLY

Write a candid out-of-office reply below. Describe your burn-out or your excitement about something outside of work that will bring you some thrills.

GET SOME FUCKING SLEEP

"You can sleep when you're dead" is the mantra of sociopaths. So much of work panic can be ameliorated by consistently good sleep, and hard work can be made better work when it's coming from a well-rested person who does not resemble a fucking zombie. Let sleep be your reward for good days and bad days by committing to going to bed at the same time every night. Wind down your screen time beforehand so your body has time to adjust, put your phone on Do Not Disturb, and lull yourself into sleep-mode. In this mini sleep journal below, describe the next few nights of sleep. How do you arrive at restfulness?

ZZZZZ...

"It will be a little messy,
BUT EMBRACE THE MESS.
It will be complicated, but
REJOICE IN THE COMPLICATIONS.
It will not be anything like what
you think it will be like,

BUT SURPRISES ARE GOOD FOR YOU.
And don't be frightened:
YOU CAN ALWAYS CHANGE YOUR MIND.
I know: I've had four careers
and three husbands."

—NORA EPHRON, 1996 WELLESLEY COLLEGE COMMENCEMENT

WORK-LIFE BALANCE *and* OTHER PRECIOUS LIES

Having it all is a tall order. The fuller your cup becomes, the closer that surface tension is to bursting, spilling your dreams all over the place.

What do you want to add to your cup?

_____

_____

_____

_____

_____

_____

What could you pull back on so that you're not too close to the breaking point?

_____

_____

_____

_____

Make a toast to the balance you can have and the things that are working well.

"Apologies have nothing to do with you. They are balloons in the sky. They may never land. They may even choke a bird."

— *YES PLEASE*, AMY POEHLER

UP, UP, AND AWAY!

Work conflicts are bound to happen. Some disagreements resolve themselves, and others spiral into a horrifying storm of frustration and perpetual dread for every time you interact with that person. When these disagreements arise and you find yourself in a space of regret, how will you feel if your attempts to quell the problem aren't well received?

_____

_____

_____

_____

_____

Can you move forward

∧∧ KNOWING IT ISN'T RESOLVED BUT ∧∧

that you have done your best to try?

_____

_____

_____

_____

_____

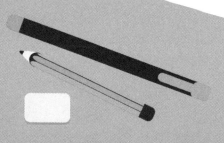

"I am notorious for making impassioned speeches about things nobody cares about."

—WHY NOT ME?, MINDY KALING

FRIENDS, CO-WORKERS, COUNTRYMEN...

Write a heartfelt speech about shit no one else cares about but you. Make it big and grand, and say what you need to say here.

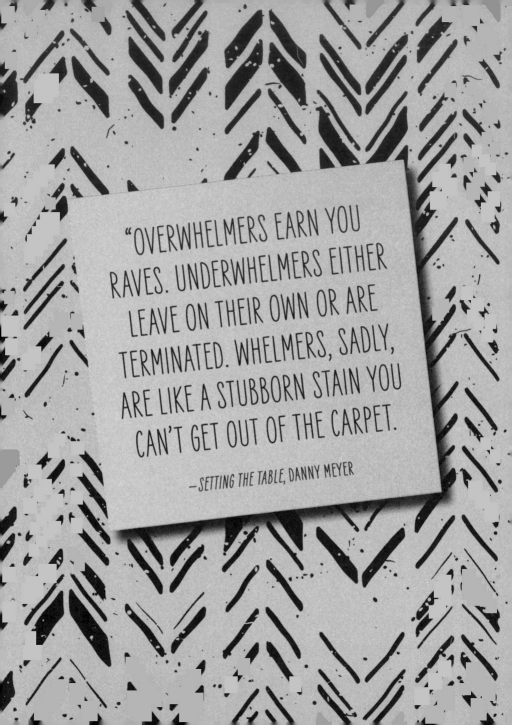

"OVERWHELMERS EARN YOU RAVES. UNDERWHELMERS EITHER LEAVE ON THEIR OWN OR ARE TERMINATED. WHELMERS, SADLY, ARE LIKE A STUBBORN STAIN YOU CAN'T GET OUT OF THE CARPET.

—*SETTING THE TABLE,* DANNY MEYER

WHELM, ACTUALLY...

What is whelming about your work life? The parts of the job that feel the most stagnant, the most out of touch with what you care about? Write them out below, and then scatter the page with colorful bits of your work that do feel fucking great. Take notice of the things that aren't working, but let yourself revel in the things that are.

 *Check out all that good!*

"FIRST YOU JUMP OFF THE CLIFF AND YOU BUILD YOUR WINGS ON THE WAY DOWN."

—RAY BRADBURY

TIME *to* SOAR

So much stress at work is brought on by risks that are just sitting there, collecting dust, when they could be leading to something great. The feeling of being stuck with your feet on the ground is overwhelming, but giving yourself a good shove can make all the difference.

What are you afraid of at work?

_____

_____

_____

_____

_____

What kinds of changes would make you feel like

A FUCKING MAJESTIC EAGLE FLYING

through the air, soaring to success?

_____

_____

_____

_____

_____

"Thank you for making time in your busy life to come in here and get in the way of mine."

—ANYA JENKINS, BUFFY THE VAMPIRE SLAYER

GOOD NEWS!
YOU ARE NOT A PUNCHING BAG!

Self-important douchebags—they're so adorable. There they are, running around in an aggressive frenzy ruining everyone's day and acting like their shit is more important than yours. In what ways has someone in your work environment taken all of their frustration out on you?

_____

_____

_____

_____

_____

Is there ever a time when their nonsense is so outlandish that it's actually funny, even if it wasn't in the moment?

_____

_____

_____

_____

_____

_____

"It Is Your Birthday."

– THE OFFICE

HOORAY, FORCED JOY *for* EVERYONE!

Work parties, cake-cutting in the break room, activities that are more soul-crushing than ice-breaking—there are so many ways to breed existential work dread!

What is the most absurd way you have been forced to bond with your colleagues?

_____

_____

_____

_____

What would have actually helped build a little kumbaya camaraderie?

_____

_____

_____

_____

_____

"And now that you don't have to be perfect, you can be good."

— *EAST OF EDEN*, JOHN STEINBECK

BURSTING BUBBLES

Imagine your career growth is made up of bubbles. As you tap the wand on the inside of the container, you gather as much of that soapy goodness as you can to prepare for what's to come. Sometimes the result is a beautiful sequence of pearlescent orbs floating into the sky, and other times, that shit *pop-pop-pops* into a sad, drippy mess. Not all bubbles are meant to keep going, and others are there to awe and inspire you to keep making more. In the bubbles below, write out the efforts you've made in the past or plan to make in the future.

Are you okay knowing that some of them will *burst*, and some of them will *float*?

"If I'm shinin', everybody
gonna shine.
Yeah, I'm goals."

—"JUICE," LIZZO

SPREAD THAT SUNSHINE, MOTHERFUCKER!

Light radiates. When you are feeling positive or successful, be generous with that light. Let it cast a glow on the people around you and bring the good energy you're feeling into each new situation.

How can you share your optimism with others?

_____

_____

_____

_____

_____

What does it feel like when someone else shares their exuberance with you?

_____

_____

_____

_____

_____

"A deep life is a good life."

— *DEEP WORK, CAL NEWPORT*

DERPY DERP DEEP

Living deeply—finding deep relaxation in your off hours, feeling deep satisfaction in your work—isn't something you just stumble into. It takes effort, focus, and dedication. Maybe this means holding off on emails until morning so you're not contaminating your personal time with work stress, or maybe it means destroying your eardrums* with a "focus" playlist on maximum volume and getting everything done before you clock out. In the columns below, write out which kinds of deep efforts you can make at work to help you gain more deep moments outside of it.

DEEPLY WORKING   DEEPLY LIVING

_____   _____

_____   _____

_____   _____

_____   _____

_____   _____

_____   _____

_____   _____

_____   _____

*Early hearing loss is no joke, folks.

"She's my friend because we both know what it's like to have people be jealous of us."

—CHER HOROWITZ, *CLUELESS*

A WORD *or* SEVERAL *on* ENVY

There are the kinds of people who appear to bounce around life, buoyantly moving from one moment of Zen to the next or from one success to another as if by accident. It is quite possible they are very lucky, very motivated, or a providential combination of both. (Or maybe they are liars, who knows!) But there are some things, maybe even many, that other people may notice about you that elicit the same levels of envy.

Instead of dwelling in envy, in what ways can you
feel happiness for that person
and their successes? In what ways can you
feel that good-good about your own?

_____

_____

_____

_____

_____

_____

_____

_____

_____

_____

_____

RECOMMENDATIONS FTW

Write your own letter of recommendation as if you were writing one for a friend or respected colleague. In the third person, write about what you appreciate about your efforts, the attitude you bring to your role, and the little things that make you pretty fucking great.

How hard is it to write
about yourself?

_____

_____

_____

_____

_____

_____

_____

Is it easier when you distance yourself a bit?

_____

_____

_____

_____

_____

_____

_____

_____

CHILL *the* FUCK OUT

Finding inner peace and serenity can be hard when everything is a fucking nightmare. Take a step back. Rather than trudging into whatever bullshit lies ahead, take a moment to breathe, collect yourself, and walk around it.

WHAT ARE THE THINGS THAT HELP YOU FEEL RELAXED?

_____

_____

_____

_____

_____

WHO OR WHAT PULLS YOU BACK AND REMINDS YOU THAT YOU CAN MAKE A TURN TOWARD TRANQUILITY?

_____

_____

_____

_____

_____

"I'm just afraid of having a tombstone that says HERE LIES A PROMISING OLD MAN."

—*INFINITE JEST*, DAVID FOSTER WALLACE

THE FUTURE is YOURS!

What is most promising about the road ahead? Small milestones or large—what are you most excited to work toward?

_____

_____

_____

_____

_____

_____

_____

What do you worry you won't get to do?

_____

_____

_____

_____

_____

_____

_____

_____

"Let me never
fall into the
VULGAR MISTAKE
OF DREAMING
that I am persecuted
whenever I am contradicted."

—RALPH WALDO EMERSON, *EMERSON IN HIS JOURNALS*

CRITICISM: A GENTLE EMBRACE

It's okay to be wrong. It's okay to disagree. When someone contradicts you or offers criticism, reel it in for a cuddle. (And none of that ass-out shit.) In what ways have you been criticized or contradicted at work that made you feel defensive?

_____

_____

_____

_____

_____

_____

[How can you *embrace that criticism*
in ways that could help or allow you to find common ground?]

_____

_____

_____

_____

_____

_____

"I wasn't a failed DJ.
I was pre-successful."

—JASON MENDOZA, *THE GOOD PLACE*

FAILURE IS JUST SUCCESS THAT'S TAKING *its* SWEET-ASS TIME

Sometimes telling children that they're very bright and will grow up to be winners is a good thing. Other times, it screws up an entire generation into thinking shit will always work out as planned.

WHEN HAS FAILURE SMACKED YOU IN THE FACE?

_____

_____

_____

_____

_____

CAN YOU TURN THAT FAILURE ON ITS HEAD AND THINK OF THE WAYS IT HELPED POINT YOU IN A BETTER DIRECTION?

_____

_____

_____

_____

_____

_____

"I believe in myself."

—SYDNEY, A CONTESTANT ON *MASTER CHEF JUNIOR* WHO KNOWS WHAT'S UP

YOU can FUCKING DO IT!

Be your own confidence booster. Imagine you're in the crowd at your own performance. What kinds of positivity can you shout at yourself from the cheap seats? What kind of encouragement will give you the energy you need to keep going?

_____

_____

_____

_____

_____

_____

_____

_____

_____

_____

_____

_____

_____

_____

_____

PROCRASTINATION: A LOVE STORY

There are procrastinators and there are the procrastinate-ees. Every procrastinator knows that the buildup of pressure and stress is TOTALLY WORTH IT, because that pile of coal is bound to yield a sparkling diamond someday. Every procrastinate-ee knows that that person is kind of an asshole, but is forced to deal with it anyway because shiny things are great.

 WHICH ONE ARE YOU?

Write a heartfelt note to the other person expressing your appreciation, frustration, or desire to do better.

_____

_____

_____

_____

_____

_____

_____

_____

_____

_____

CONGRATULATIONS!
you SURVIVED TODAY.

Miracles can happen. Big or small, write about what got you through the day. Even if most of the day royally sucked, focus on the friendly face, the funny joke, or the pleasant treat that made it a little bit better.

WHAT ABOUT THAT MOMENT MADE YOU FEEL GOOD?

_____

_____

_____

_____

_____

_____

_____

_____

_____

_____

OOPSIES!

WELL, FUCK. Mistakes at work abound, and while some of them are the *you're-definitely-fired* kind, others are pretty funny after the wave of embarrassment has washed back out to sea. Whether it's a reply-all gone horribly awry or a blunder that affected the task at hand, write about it here to give yourself some laughs.

_____

_____

_____

_____

_____

_____

_____

_____

_____

_____

_____

_____

_____

AAAHAHAHAHAHA!!!!!

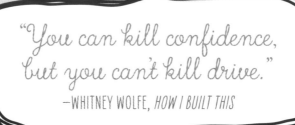

"You can kill confidence,
but you can't kill drive."
—WHITNEY WOLFE, *HOW I BUILT THIS*

IMMORTAL AMBITION

Confidence is capricious. When you have it, you feel like you're on top of the world, but when it's taken away, it feels like a shadowy hell-hole of a void. When your confidence is on life support, what keeps you moving?

_____

_____

_____

_____

_____

_____

_____

_____

_____

_____

_____

 Allow the determination you feel for tasks, GOAL TRAJECTORY, OR WORK RELATIONSHIPS TO REINVIGORATE YOU, even if your confidence is still on the mend.

"OH, YEAH!"

–THE KOOL-AID GUY

"AM I IN A CULT?" AND OTHER QUESTIONS YOU MAY ASK YOURSELF AT WORK

Oh, the hive mind. A helpful resource when you need information en masse, but when your company's mission statement starts flashing across your nightmares or you bleed for your office bowling team, you know something's up. What flavor Kool-Aid does your job serve?

_____

_____

_____

_____

Is it super tasty, or do you need to

pour it into a plant

when nobody's watching?

_____

_____

_____

_____

"A hug is like a strangle you haven't finished yet."

—COPERNICUS THE MONKEY, *THE BLOGGESS*

SAYONARA, SMOTHERING COLLEAGUE!

Workplace friendships are amazing. They build you up, make you better, and create a sense of home in a place that is decidedly not. Workplace smothering is another beast entirely. Who is the co-worker who's always up in your space, who asks too many personal questions, or who constantly needs to interject their opinion into every facet of your day?

_____

_____

_____

_____

_____

ARE THERE DIPLOMATIC WAYS TO CREATE SPACE BETWEEN YOU?

_____

_____

_____

_____

_____

MAKE THEM LOOSEN THAT GRIP SO YOU HAVE SOME BREATHING ROOM!

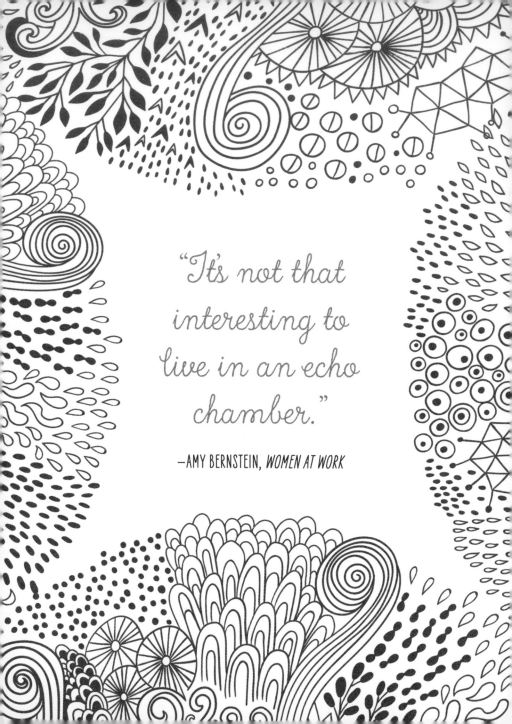

"It's not that interesting to live in an echo chamber."

—AMY BERNSTEIN, *WOMEN AT WORK*

VOICES, *not* VICES

Cooperative voices, unite! It's validating to feel as though the world is right on its axis, that success is imminent, and that being a freaking genius is your forte. But if your positions are habitually being validated rather than challenged or if the ideas you hear are a chorus, it's possible that there are voices going unheard. When have you felt like you were in an echo chamber?

_____

_____

_____

_____

_____

WHAT KINDS OF VOICES WOULD HAVE DISRUPTED THOSE ECHOES, FOR BETTER OR WORSE?

_____

_____

_____

_____

_____

_____

PUT IT IN THE SUGGESTION BOX

Put some notes in your personal suggestion box. Encourage yourself to be more confident, inspire yourself to learn new skills, and pop in some reminders to stop doing whatever it is you do that drives other people crazy—like butt-dialing them on off hours or being a fucking micromanager. Get real with your suggestions, but garnish them with positive twists so you feel motivated to follow through.

STFU!

DON'T BE A DICK!

GREAT JOB!

WELL DONE!

"FEEDBACK"

"What I hear when I am being yelled at is people caring loudly at me."

—LESLIE KNOPE, *PARKS AND RECREATION*

WOES THERE!

Yell out your frustrations here. Go all-CAPS ape-shit and let your howls reverberate across the expanse of this page.

ENJOY!

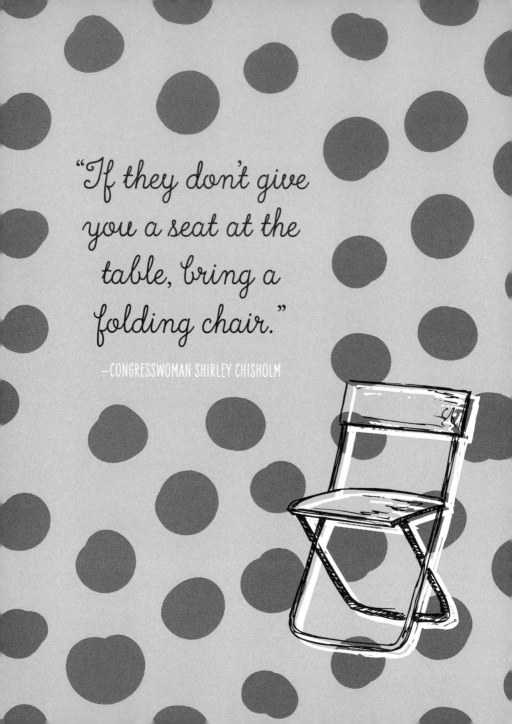

"If they don't give you a seat at the table, bring a folding chair."

—CONGRESSWOMAN SHIRLEY CHISHOLM

PULL UP a SEAT

Work is no picnic, but like picnics, there is a serious fucking
shortage of seating in any given field. Bias in the workplace and
the reality that those at the top have the power to shut out
others are hard pills to swallow. When have you been kept from a
seat at the table, or watched it being kept from someone else?

_____

_____

_____

_____

_____

{ HOW CAN YOU TRY TO POP OPEN A
JUMP SEAT FOR YOURSELF OR FOR OTHERS? }

_____

_____

_____

_____

_____

_____

_____

"What is money anyway?
IT'S JUST PAPER THAT SOME KING ON A
mountain said was worth something.
GOLD I UNDERSTAND, IT'S SHINY."

—NICK MILLER, *NEW GIRL*

THAT'S RICH

Jumping into a pile of gold like Scrooge McDuck sure sounds nice, but there are pitfalls to making it the focus of your happiness (including, but not limited to, the fact that it would be very, very painful). Build your emotional wealth while you work toward your financial goals. In the left-hand column, make a list of the parts of your life where you feel emotionally wealthy. In the right-hand column, make a list of your financial objectives and how you can inch toward them.

"SHARING REWARDS THE WEAK."

—STEPHEN COLBERT, *THE COLBERT REPORT*

HELPING HANDS!

Some people are helpers. Other people climb up the corporate ladder and chuck projectiles down at everyone below them to crush the competition. To each his own! But at some point or another, you've been helped. Whether in a big way or a small way, how has someone helped you at work?

_____

_____

_____

_____

_____

WHEN HAVE YOU LAUNCHED PROJECTILES?

_____

_____

_____

_____

_____

_____

_____

"Most of the time, when you get rejected, the main reason is not you. It's not me. It's us."

—ADAM GRANT, *WORKLIFE*

I'M NOT FIRED, I QUIT!

Jobs are not unlike dating. There's the happy, symbiotic relationship that makes you both better; the job that ghosts you by letting your resume go unrequited; and there's the one that's toxic as fuck. In an employment situation that turned sour or didn't go anywhere at all, was it a one-sided heartbreak, or were you just not meant for each other?

⟫⟶ WHAT WOULD BE YOUR IDEAL WORK MATCH? ⟵《

NSFW

HUMAN RESOURCES!

Not-safe-for-work moments run the gamut. There's the hilarious kind that you can't help but come back to every time you need a laugh, and there's the fucking horrifying sort that probably requires a legal team. What are the most bizarre, out-of-line things you remember falling under this umbrella?

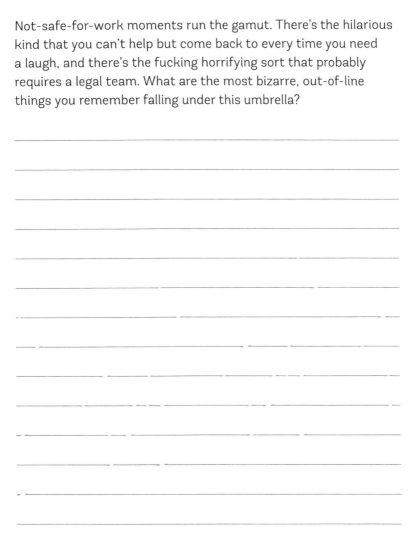

"What we achieve inwardly will change outer reality."

—PLUTARCH

MIRROR MANIFESTING

Confidence is yours for the taking. Let your favorite motivational mantra float through your mind for a minute or two each morning. Stand in front of the mirror as you do it, take a deep breath, and repeat it aloud. Feel that surge of energy flow through you as you go out into the workday to kick ass. How does this feel?

_____

_____

_____

_____

_____

_____

Does it feel different each day?

_____

_____

_____

_____

_____

_____

_____

Sift Through the rocky shit to Find What's Golden.

GOLD RUSH

Work is a constant search for something bright within the grit. More often than not, it will be difficult and laborious (it's fucking work, after all) but the search for something positive can reveal a glittering tomorrow.

WHAT FLECKS OF GOLD DO YOU FIND IN YOUR JOB, OR DO YOU SOMEDAY HOPE TO FIND?

ZEN AS F*CK AT WORK

Workplace serenity is a personal persuit. Stock up on the
soothing efforts that work for you, lest you find yourself yo-yoing
in a corner because the listicle your boss read on "the Net" said
it was the hip new way to reduce stress. What efforts make you
feel the most at peace, whether it's letting go of other people's
bullshit, creating a space of solitude at certain points in the day,
or finding support in others?

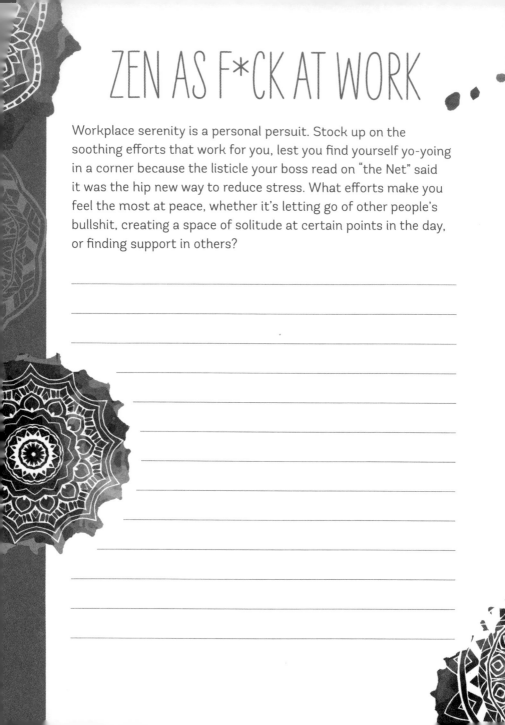

ACKNOWLEDGMENTS

MY WORKPLACE JOY would not be possible without Holly Schmidt, Allan Penn, Bruce Lubin, Aimee Chase, Katie Jennings Campbell, Jennifer Leight, Marisa Bartlett, Joanna Williams, and Melissa Gerber. Thank you for making each day more fun than the one before, for being relentlessly encouraging, and for being infinitely inspiring to work with. To Andy Martin, Nichole Argyres, Courtney Littler, Meryl Gross, Amelie Littell, and the whole team at St. Martin's who bring stellar books into the world and who are a delight to work with every day. Big hugs and love to my remote friends who make their offices in every corner of the world or any coffee shop with a decent WiFi connection.

ABOUT THE AUTHOR

Monica Sweeney is a writer and editor. Her books include
Zen as F*ck, *Let That Sh*t Go*, and *Find Your F*cking Happy*,
among others. She lives in Boston, Massachusetts.